SCHOLASTIC
TRUE OR FALSE

Rocks & Minerals

BY MELVIN AND GILDA BERGER

Text copyright © 2010 by Melvin and Gilda Berger
All rights reserved. Published by Scholastic Inc., *Publishers since 1920.*
SCHOLASTIC and associated logos are trademarks and/or
registered trademarks of Scholastic Inc.

ISBN 978-0-545-20205-3

10 9 8 7 6 5 4 3 2 1   10 11 12 13 14

Printed in the U.S.A.   40
First printing, November 2010
Original book design by Nancy Sabato
Composition by Kay Petronio

Rocks are made of minerals.

TRUE OR FALSE?

TRUE! All rocks are made of minerals.

Minerals are hard substances that come from the Earth and were never alive. A few kinds of rocks, such as marble and limestone, are made of only one mineral. But most rocks are made of two, three, or more minerals. Granite, for example, is a rock that consists mainly of three minerals — quartz, feldspar, and mica.

There are more than 4,000 known kinds of minerals

Crystals are found inside minerals.

TRUE OR FALSE?

TRUE! Crystals are solids found inside minerals that give them their shape.

Crystals have many smooth, flat surfaces that meet at sharp angles. The simplest crystals look like cubes. Complex crystals have many more sides — some parallel, some not. The exact shape of the mineral depends on how and where the crystals formed.

Salt is made up of halite crystals.

Earth is a big
ball of rock.
TRUE
OR
FALSE?

TRUE! Earth is made up of layers of rock.

We walk on the hard outer layer, or crust. Below the crust is the thick mantle. In some places, the mantle is so hot that the rock actually melts and becomes a liquid, called magma. Beneath the mantle is the outer core of melted rock, which surrounds a solid inner core that is Earth's center. Scientists think that the core may contain the metals iron and nickel.

Earth's rocky crust is under oceans, soil, or ice.

All rocks
are gray.

TRUE
OR
FALSE?

FALSE! Many rocks are gray — but a rock can be any color or mix of colors.

A rock's color depends on the minerals that make up the rock. Some rocks contain just one kind of mineral, so they are one color, such as blue or yellow. Other rocks are like granite. It is made up of minerals with several different colors: white or pink (feldspar), gray (quartz), and black (mica).

Long ago, artists made colorful paint from crushed rocks.

All rocks are hard.

TRUE or FALSE?

FALSE! Not all rocks are hard.

The hardness comes from the minerals that make up the rock. Soapstone is a soft rock. It contains the softest mineral, talc. You can easily shape soapstone or other rocks made of soft minerals. Emery is a hard rock that contains several very hard minerals.

Emery is often ground up and used to polish gems or metals.

All rocks are formed the same way.

TRUE OR FALSE?

FALSE!

Rocks are formed in three main ways. First, rocks made of magma that has cooled and hardened are called igneous rocks. Second, those made from tiny bits of rock, or sediment, are sedimentary rocks. And third, rocks whose characteristics have been changed by heat and pressure become metamorphic rocks.

Most of Earth's crust is igneous rock.

Igneous rocks can form under the ground. TRUE OR FALSE?

TRUE! Magma sometimes cools under Earth's surface and forms igneous rocks.

The liquid magma beneath the crust sometimes turns solid between layers of rock. Igneous rocks are also formed when magma flows out through a volcano to Earth's surface. As the liquid rock, now called lava, reaches the surface, it is cooled by the air. In time, it hardens into solid rock.

Layers of cooled lava can build up to form mountains.

All igneous
rocks sink
in water.

TRUE
OR
FALSE?

FALSE! Pumice is an igneous rock that floats.

As the pumice rock forms inside a volcano, it becomes full of tiny air bubbles. The quick-cooling pumice traps the bubbles inside the rock. This makes the rock lighter than water — and able to float.

Builders add pumice to concrete to make lightweight building material.

500

400

300

200

100

All igneous rocks are rough to the touch.

TRUE OR FALSE?

FALSE! Igneous rocks can be smooth or rough.

It all depends on whether the magma cools and hardens quickly or slowly. Obsidian, for example, is formed from magma that cools very quickly. Crystals do not have time to form. This makes obsidian as smooth as glass. Gabbro, on the other hand, is made from magma that cools slowly. This rock generally contains many large crystals. You can identify gabbro by its very rough and coarse feel.

Gabbro can be found on the Moon.

Sedimentary rocks usually form in water. **TRUE OR FALSE?**

TRUE! Many sedimentary rocks form at the bottom of rivers or oceans.

Rain, wind, ice, and flowing water wear away rocks. The pieces of rock, along with bits of sand and mud, are called sediment. In time, the sediment settles on the bottom of the ocean or river. Layers and layers of sediment pile up, higher and higher. The layers press down so hard that eventually the soft sediment turns into solid sedimentary rock.

The sedimentary rocks at the bottom of the Grand Canyon are about two billion years old.

Sedimentary
rocks may
contain
fossils.

TRUE
OR
FALSE?

TRUE! Almost all fossils are found in sedimentary rocks.

Fossils are the remains or traces of plants and animals that lived millions of years ago. Most fossils form when plants or animals get trapped in sand or mud that hardens into sedimentary rock. Over many years, the soft parts rot away. Hard shells, bones, and teeth remain and become fossils.

Many dinosaur fossils have been foun
in the United States.

Some
sedimentary
rocks are
made from
plants.

TRUE
OR
FALSE?

TRUE! Coal is made of plants that grew in ancient swamps.

The plants died and rotted. They were buried under layers of sand, rocks, mud, and other dead plants. Over millions of years, the layers squeezed the plant material. It hardened into narrow bands of black coal. Today, miners dig deep into Earth's crust to remove the coal.

Anthracite, the coal that burns best, is found deepest under the ground.

Sedimentary rocks sometimes form in caves.

TRUE OR FALSE?

TRUE! Sedimentary rock builds up on certain cave floors and ceilings.

This buildup occurs when water drips through caves formed of limestone. As the water passes through the rock, it picks up bits of the mineral calcite. The water evaporates and leaves the calcite behind. In time, the calcite accumulates — rising up from the cave floor or hanging down from the ceiling.

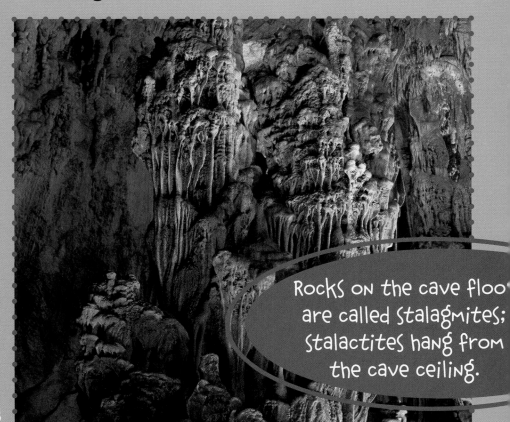

Rocks on the cave floor are called stalagmites; stalactites hang from the cave ceiling.

Both sedimentary and igneous rocks can become a third kind of rock.

TRUE OR FALSE?

TRUE! A third type of rock, called metamorphic rock, comes from sedimentary and igneous rocks.

Great heat and pressure within the Earth gradually change the shape and hardness of these rocks. The changed rocks are called metamorphic rocks. Marble is a hard metamorphic rock good for carving. It was once the soft sedimentary rock limestone.

Marble from pure limestone is white in color.

Rocks last
forever.
TRUE
OR
FALSE?

FALSE! Rocks can last a long time — but not forever.

Various forces in nature — air, sun, wind, and rain — eventually break rocks down into smaller and smaller bits. Flowing rivers and ocean waves bang rocks against each other and break them apart. Winds blow sand against rocks and wear bits away. When water freezes into ice inside the crack of a rock, it can split the rock apart.

Rocks that break can become other sedimentary rocks

Growing plants can break rocks apart.

TRUE OR FALSE?

TRUE! Plants that take root in rocks can split them.

Bits of soil sometimes collect on rocks. Seeds may fall there. Plants, including trees, can sprout. The growing plants apply slow, steady pressure on the rocks. In time, the roots and trunk may become strong enough to break the rocks apart. Over many, many years, the rocks may crumble and wash away.

Erosion happens when rocks are worn away by wind or water.

Some minerals are very valuable. TRUE OR FALSE?

TRUE! Diamonds, emeralds, rubies, and Sapphires are among the most precious minerals of all.

These minerals, which form in rocks, are called gemstones. They have some of the most beautiful colors found in nature. Gemstones are also very rare and hard to find. Miners dig for them in both igneous and metamorphic rock.

Of the more than 4,000 known minerals, only 15 or So form most gemstones.

Diamond is a soft mineral.

TRUE or FALSE?

FALSE! Diamond is the hardest mineral of all.

It is also among the oldest. Most diamonds form deep in the Earth under extreme heat and pressure over many millions of years. Some formed up to three billion years ago. Light beams bounce off the inside of a cut diamond to give the stone its sparkle.

The only thing that can scratch a diamond is another diamond.

Metals are
not found
in rocks.

TRUE
OR
FALSE?

FALSE! Some rocks contain metals.

These rocks are called ores. Workers dig the ores out of the ground and remove the metals. Aluminum, for example, comes from an ore called bauxite. The workers use giant shovels to scoop the bauxite from huge open pits. Trucks then carry the bauxite to plants where the pure aluminum is removed.

Aluminum is the most common metal in Earth's crust.

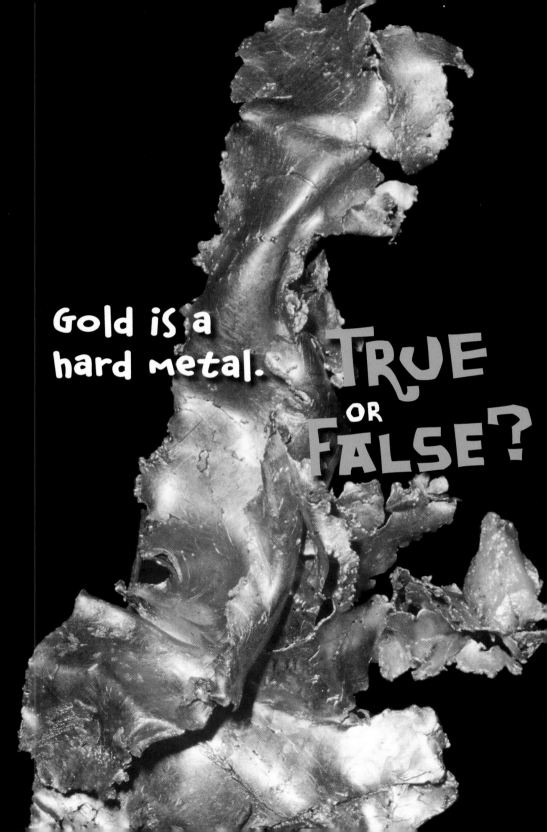

Gold is a
hard metal. **TRUE OR FALSE?**

FALSE! Gold is one of the softest metals.

People love gold for its soft, beautiful yellow glow. This metal forms in igneous rock that is removed from deposits found under the ground. Most of the gold is made into jewelry. During California's gold rush in 1849, many people panned for gold. They looked for bits of the metal in the sand at the bottom of flowing streams.

Gold that was mined in ancient time still looks bright and shiny today.

Rocks fall to
Earth from
Space.

TRUE
OR
FALSE?

TRUE! Space rocks sometimes crash into the surface of Earth.

These rocks from outer space are called meteorites. They are made of rock or metal or a mixture of both. Most rocks from outer space explode and break up into small pieces when entering the Earth's atmosphere. A few are large enough to crash into Earth's surface and make small pits. Some giant ones leave huge holes, or craters, behind.

The famous Meteor Crater in Arizona was created by a meteorite 50,000 years ago.

MOON rocks are NOT like earth rocks. TRUE OR FALSE?

FALSE! Rocks from the Moon resemble earth rocks.

Astronauts have collected rocks on the Moon for testing on Earth. The moon rocks were found to be very similar to earth rocks. One big difference is the age of the rocks. The ones from the Moon are older (4.5 billion years) than the oldest earth rocks (3.8 billion years).

Meteorites have been found on the Moon and the planet Mars.

Index